Protected by the Promises

Original Poetry
by
Jo Anne Burkhart McKinney

Copyright ©2010
by Jo Anne Burkhart McKinney

ISBN# 978-0-9830852-0-1

McKinney, Jo Anne Burkhart
Protected by the Promises
Original Poetry

All rights reserved. No part of this book may be printed or reproduced without express written permission of the author. Individual poems or lines may, however, be read aloud to a group or congregation.

Published by Jo Anne Burkhart McKinney
PO Box 198
Sandyville, Ohio 44671

Printed in the U.S.A.
GORDON PRINTING
Strasburg, Ohio

Preface
Pathways…Promises…Protection

I chose as the title for this book <u>Protected by the Promises</u> because my first little book of poetry was titled <u>Pathways and Promises</u>. All these 26 years later, I am much further down the pathway and God's promises have protected me through all the experiences.

Through 36 years of marriage to a man who allowed alcohol to ruin his life, 26 years of caring for a handicapped daughter, 29 years of teaching, and more than 20 years of praying to live long enough to see a drug-addicted, alcoholic son straighten out, the Lord protected me. He gave me strength when I had none of my own, patience to cope, grace to persevere, and deeper faith as I struggled and grew closer to Him. He saw me through financial crises, a dissolution, kept me safe in transit, gave me comfort as I buried each of my children and their father, and continued to grant me peace and shower me with blessings.

Among the greatest blessings have been close friends of many years, my three grandchildren, and a new husband of great faith and humility. This marriage is a daily joy and a grateful walk together with our Lord.

Believing God's promises is what sustains me on the pathways, for no matter how rocky or steep the path may be, no matter how crowded or lonely, how short or long…He is there to protect me and help me along.

I invite you to walk with me on the pathway. As you read these poems, please identify with the ones that resemble your own path; enjoy or learn from the parts of my walk that may be different from yours. Please note the date at the end of each poem and realize that they span a number of years and they refer to specific times in my life.

Focus, if you will, on the promises that prevail, the parts of the journey that all Christians know..that God's promises and protection are real and true and are available to each of us.

DEDICATION
I dedicate this book to my Lord Jesus Christ.
It is my prayer that these poems will inspire,
help and reach people for Him.

IN MEMORY
I honor the memory of my children
who have gone before me to be with the Lord.
They were the inspiration for a number of these poems.

Amy Jo Burkhart	Brett Allen Burkhart
Feb. 21, 1970 -	Mar. 20, 1966 -
Dec. 29, 1995	June 4, 2009

THANKS
Many thanks to those who have encouraged me
to continue writing, who have graciously acknowledged
the sharing of my poems, who have requested that
this book be published.

Protected by the Promises---

---in Trials and Joys of Life

….ye shall weep and lament, but the world
shall rejoice; and ye shall be sorrowful,
but your sorrow shall be turned into joy.
--John 16:20 KJV

Recipe for a "Seasoned" Life

Life: a blend of ingredients, recipes of our choosing;
A selection of seasonings pleasing our taste.
Bland, pungent, tasteful, sweet, sour, using
Each moment carefully; no thyme to waste.

Renewal in springtimes of coriander flurry,
Youthful activity basil with green;
Oregano-flavored with touches of curry,
Childhood's a pleasant, innocent scene.

Parsleyed adventures stir summer's glow;
Peppered with learning, baked in the sun;
Rosemary leisure kneading to flow,
Teen, young adult years too quickly done.

Gingerly folding to saffron Septembers,
Autumn years more deliberately greet;
Bright mustard melodies fondly remembered;
Middle-age memories so cinnamon sweet.

Powdery winter hills, sugared with snow,
Salted roads traveled at much slower pace;
Minted treasures discovered, eat in or to go,
Accepting the outcome with wisdom and grace.

Seasonings of life include bitter and biting,
Candied and luscious, sprinkled with zest;
Attitude flavors each dish, inviting
A pleasurable palate of life at its best!

-2010

Who is ME?

Let myself go?   No.   I'm never really free to be me.
Who am I, anyway?

It seems, each day, that I'm so much involved
With problems needing solved,
With meeting others' needs,
Which nearly always leads
To no time for me to be anything....except tired.

When I do have energy to be fired about something,
Then—you got it! The time's not right—that shot it!

Would I know what I want if I had time to hunt
And space to explore? Would I search for more than I've had?
Would that be bad? Is what I have good?
Maybe I should just forget about myself. Yet, the more I know
That's desirable, the more I'll go on thinking of ways
To find time in days to try to pursue what I want to do.

Then, what about those who believe I chose to do
What I'm doing? If I start pursuing the things I want most,
Will that leave a host of problems for them?
Will their troubles stem from my change of view?
Will it be my fault, too, if they fall flat because I moved?
Has it behooved me to question at all who I am?
Can I call myself me when I'm always expected to be
In demand, on command?

I'll just keep a wall around my heart
So it won't fall apart. I'll learn to stop thinking
About all the drinking in of life I am missing.
As long as I'm kissing a sweet experience once in a while,
I'll smile.... and go on being what you are seeing:

A flesh and blood robot programmed to a lot
Of being what others think I should be.

Who is ME?   -1989

When Problems Pass Your Way

Life seems doubly precious
    after problems pass your way;
You realize how people care
    by what they do and say.
If you really need a helping hand,
    suddenly it's there,
And all your Christian friends join
    in the miracle of prayer.

It matters not how heavy
    the burdens seem to weigh;
There's more hope in tomorrow,
    more light in each new day.
God doesn't send His children
    any more than they can bear,
But He teaches them with trials
    that they need His loving care.

Yes, the sky seems so much bluer
    after it's been gray,
And life is so much dearer
    when problems pass your way.
For it is through the burdens
    that we show how much we care
And we know that life's more precious
    when we've had a cross to bear.

We sometimes live in selfishness
    when everything's "O.K.",
But we show our friends we love them
    when problems pass their way.

        -1970

CLUTTERED MARRIAGES

Treasures—Trinkets—Objects—
They clutter up our lives;
They build a worldly barrier
Between husbands and wives.

Instead of working to develop
Better communication,
They concentrate on the next "want"
Of their accumulation.

And somewhere in the process
Some precious things are lost,
And, sadly, often much too late
Is realized --- the cost.

The listening to each other
That marriages should share,
The simple, tender gestures
Of showing that you care

Are sacrificed for busy-ness
In the name of "necessary"
And shoved into the background
Is the reason that you marry.

Wake up! Oh, wives and husbands!
What are you thinking of?
You must take time to express,
Share and appreciate your love.

There's no happiness in objects,
For take them all away
And what is left is all you'll have:
Your feelings --- and this day.

So if you do love each other,
Clean out your mind and heart:
Sweep the clutter from your lives,
And make a brand new start!

-1982

COLLECTING

As I look around me
It should not astound me
That my existence is saturated
With items that infatuated
My fancy to collect.

So, I am surrounded
And occasionally dumbfounded
To realize to what extent
This adding to each group has meant.
The urge, I can´t reject.

I tell myself I´ll add no more;
I´m running out of room to store
Another thing, another place.
I´m simply running out of space
To add another shelf.

I´m not willing to make confession
That this ``collecting´´ is an obsession.
``It´s just things that I enjoy´´
Is an excuse that I employ
To satisfy myself.

I arrange the groups so nicely;
Each article placed so precisely
In curios, on shelves or walls,
From flea markets or antique malls
Or family or friends.

I promise I will add no more,
To downsize my increasing store
Of groups of various stuff.
My ears are ringing. ``O.K.! Enough!´´
Alas, collecting never ends.

-2003

Who Is the Judge?

As mere humans, who are we
To determine what life is worth?
The quality of existence is not
Designed purely by birth.

Tabulation of time spent here
Measured not in years may be,
But in influence on others
Leading to eternity.

Which is the greater loss, I ask,
A damaged brain, a body lame,
Or full potential wasted
With only self to blame?

A person with disability
A true blessing can be
To those who take for granted
Or those who fail to see

That perfection's unattainable
For any of us here,
So perhaps we should concentrate
On what we hold most dear.

Time spent with those we care about,
A precious, innocent smile,
Joys derived from sharing
Make moments so worthwhile.

Giving, not just taking,
Being there for others
Is what connects mankind in ways
To make them truly brothers.

We can, if we allow it,
Learn more from those with less;
Let God give life and take it,
Having faith that He will bless.

-2010

Life…A Dance Marathon

Life is a dance marathon…
    You have to hear the music
        and learn the steps.
One should practice regularly
    to be ready for the big contests.

Some instructors are better than others,
    but you can learn from them all.

Once in a while
    you are out of step;
        Sometimes you trip
            over your own feet,
                or lose your balance.

Then, there's the search
    for the perfect partner.

Learning new steps together,
    you can make up a new dance
        of your very own.

As you waltz across the dance hall of life,
    you will know when
        they are playing your song.

When the marathon is over
    and you take your last bow…

        the band will play on…

-1993

CAUTION: DETOUR

THE SIGN AHEAD IS MARKED DETOUR
WITH AN ARROW POINTING RIGHT;
THE DESTINATION CAN'T BE SEEN
FOR IT IS OUT OF SIGHT.

SO, THE ROAD THAT YOU WERE TRAVELING
IS TEMPORARILY CLOSED FOR REPAIR,
AND YOUR LIFE HAS BEEN RE-ROUTED
THOUGH RIGHT NOW YOU DON'T KNOW WHERE.

THE NEW BRIDGE COULD BE STRONGER,
THE NEW ROUTE A BETTER ROAD
THOUGH THE DETOUR'S INCONVENIENT
AND, AT TIMES, A HEAVY LOAD.

IF YOU'RE PATIENT ON THE DETOUR,
THERE'LL BE MUCH TO REALIZE;
THERE'S NEW SCENERY, NEW PLEASURES,
SEEN THROUGH NEWLY-OPENED EYES.

AND, SOMETIMES IT IS LIFE'S DETOURS
THAT BRING THE BEST TO US
WHICH WE NEVER WOULD DISCOVER
IF THERE HADN'T BEEN A FUSS.

IF FAMILIAR ROUTES STAY OPEN,
WE DON'T TRY NEW ROADS TO SEE
THAT THE NEW WAY MAY BE BETTER,
AND, PERHAPS, WAS MEANT TO BE.

-1990

THE MOON IN CANCUN

How can it be? The very same moon
That I saw in Ohio looks down on Cancun?
High foam-capped waves atop water azure clear
Rolling onto white sand. . a lullaby to hear.

How do you think that the rising, hot sun
Warming those beaches could be the same one
Back home in winter, barely showing its face?
This world of ours is an awesome place.

Beautiful bronze skin of native people there;
Languages so different; smiles everywhere.
Cultures diverse, yet some common bond
Connects mankind like a magic wand.

Things about each other we don't understand;
Yet we offer in friendship an outstretched hand.
We visit there. .or they visit here
Under same sunshine or moonbeams clear.

From the same sky come raindrops or snow,
Sunbeams or clouds, wherever we go.
We think we're so distant from all that is home
As we travel this earth to venture and roam

But twenty-two hundred miles away
The very same moon
That I left in Ohio
Appeared in Cancun!

-1991

Suffer the Little Children

Dear Lord, when You said, "Suffer the little children to come to me,"
Little did we comprehend what "suffering" could be.
I never realized it could mean that they would be in pain;
That many of them in their beds will not get up again.

It makes us suffer, too, Lord, to see the children ill,
But we know that Your hand contains the power to still
The raging angry waves of fever and disease
And if we put our faith in You our minds will be at ease.

These precious little people can't begin to understand
The realities of grief and pain which dwell across a land.
I pray that all the doctors, nurses, aides and parents, too,
Can trust enough to know for sure what faith in You can do.

For we indeed see miracles of healing every day;
In thankfulness we offer gratitude each time we pray.
I'm not asking to understand the grace Your love imparts.
If you don't heal their bodies, Lord, then welcome loving hearts.

–1975

Some Way to Walk

Bless my legs and bless my knees,
Dear Jesus, bless my braces please.

    And bless my walker standing there
    And my brand new shiny blue wheelchair

        And thank you for a voice to talk
        To thank you for some way to walk.

-1979

The Vicarious Gardener
(In memory of Betty Hydrick)

Betty was a special woman who spent many years in a wheelchair following an accident. She never stopped witnessing for the Lord and was an inspiration and a dear friend to so many.

She looked out of the window and appraised
How flowers could adorn the bank beyond,
A weeping cherry tree to set it off,
A garden planted by her eyes and mind.

I'm sure she longed in quiet solitude
To be on her knees with dirt and seeds,
To make the garden as she saw it there
Become not imagined, but reality.

She little knew, however, that each day
She planted inspiration in her friends,
That, watered with her tears of suffering,
Grew flowers of greater beauty in the end.

Blossoms of perseverance bloomed
As storms of life sometimes bent them low,
But, indomitable, they would return,
Evidence of spirit strong to show.

Buds of hope sprung up when needed most;
Faith bloomed throughout the seasons long;
The fragrance of a life we'll ne'er forget
Will linger in this garden like a song.

-2000

Parody

To Helen
By Edgar Allan Poe

Helen, Thy beauty is to me
Like those Nicean barks of yore
That gently, o'er a perfumed sea,
The weary, way-worn wanderer bore
To his own native shore.

On desperate seas long wont to roam
Thy hyacinth hair, Thy classic face,
Thy Naiad airs have brought me home
To the glory that was Greece,
And the grandeur that was Rome.

Lo! In yon brilliant window niche
How statue-like I see Thee stand,
The agate lamp within Thy hand!
Ah, Psyche, from the regions which
Are Holy Land!

To Bacon
By Jo Anne B. McKinney

Bacon, Thy taste will be to me
Like those crisp slices of before
That, lying on a lettuce leaf,
A juicy, red tomato bore
And mayonnaise, what's more.

On brown'ed bread thou wilt not roam.
Thy lean, lithe look, thy tempting air
Thy odors permeate my home,
Sizzling in the glorious Grease,
Giving off that grand aRoma.

Lo! On yon salad plate on which
How luscious-like I see thee stand,
I reach out for thee with my hand!
Ah! Thy existence does, Sandwich,
Make eating grand!

-1963

Survival of Truth

Just as I can't begin to understand
what an African-American experiences
in thinking about slavery

or the flashbacks of
a Vietnam veteran
as scenes of atrocities
rewind behind the eyes

Neither can I comprehend the agony
of the Holocaust survivor.

That there is no justification for the events
to make them "worth the sacrifice"
intensifies the pain, I'm sure.

The inspiration of it all seems to be
in the strength of the human spirit
to not only survive,
but to reach out to others through the pain
with the true story
that in keeping the facts alive,
any attempts at a second holocaust
may be put to death
by the reality
of Truth.

-1997

Tell the Story? Why?

What's inside must find a way
From darkest night to light of day.
So, those whose lives were stripped of glory
Feel compelled to tell their story.

Even in the darkest hour
Some knew there was a higher power
Whose grace would serve to see them through,
Helping them do what they must do.

So through it all they persevered
Although the enemy they feared.
Strength was ebbing; time so slow,
Seeing ones that they loved, go.

Feelings mattered not at all
To the watchers of the wall.
Orders given and obeyed;
People staunch, and yet afraid.

For no good reason, millions killed;
Voices of tomorrow stilled.
Those surviving closed the door
Of hearts hoping to hurt no more.

Time's perspective touched the pain
In hearts and minds where it remained,
Finally bringing some relief
As form was given to their grief.

The stories, diaries, poems, songs,
Letters, drawings, brought along
Not really purpose to their pain,
But hope it won't occur again.

So listen carefully, all of you;
Old and young, gentile and Jew,
The only preventer known as yet:
To be sure the future not forget.

{Written at a class on the holocaust}-1997

A Revelation

Little children hiding,
Families split in parts;
Many futures riding
A question mark of hearts.

Parents rent in anguish
Regarding the unknown;
Helpless, lacking answers,
Feeling so alone.

Brutal acts enacted
Viciously in hate;
Genocide exacted
At overwhelming rate.

Atrocities prolific;
Spirits rose and fell
As happenings horrific
Created living hell.

Survivors somehow existed
Through intervening years;
Now they are enlisted
To tell their tale of tears.

-1997

[written for a class on the holocaust]

Protected by the Promises---

---in Learning

How blessed is the man who finds wisdom
and the man who gains understanding.
--Proverbs 3:13 NAS

From a teacher...

PRESCHOOL

Thank you for loving your child enough
To put him in our care;
To let him be away from you
These many hours we've shared.

Thank you for the training
You have given her at home
That we could work together
To help her learn and grow.

He leaves this class a little taller
Than when he first began,
A little stronger, much more social,
Doing more of what he can.

It has been a precious privilege
To work nearer to her goals:
And we all have grown in some way
In the heartbeat of our souls.
                              -1983

HIGH SCHOOL
Thank you..
For loaning your child to me
For 40 minutes a day;
I hope I'll be able to help him
Somehow along life's way.
I'll show her wonderful words to use
To express her feelings well;
I'll take her to faraway places,
And she'll be able to tell
Of other people and cultures and times
She'd otherwise not have known,
But for stories, novels, plays and poems
She now can call her own.
I hope he'll be richer for being here;
That he'll someday realize
It takes a range of subjects and knowledge
To make a person wise.
His adventures in his classes
Will be memorable in some way:
My hope is that he'll use what he learns
In this 40 minutes a day!
                    -1992

Students of Today

When it comes to grammar, they stammer.
They don't realize they really need to read.
When you ask them to write, it's a fight.
If there's no remote or screen, it's not seen.

Yet they need basic understanding
If a job they will be landing;
Life is not all fun and games,
So we call learning by other names.

Collaborative, cooperative, group, peer
Fall upon the listening ear.
Responsible, accountable, respect
Seem to be sentenced to neglect.

What's the answer, teachers ask,
To entice students to meet the task?
The simple fact still remains:
Knowledge is necessary for gains.

Motivation to acquire knowledge
To be effective in work or college
Begins with learning what you need
So in the future you'll succeed.

So, students, Listen to instructions.
Learn to analyze and make deductions.
Read and write and study and learn
So self-respect and confidence you will earn.

-2002

A TEACHER'S ROLE

A new school year—an open book;
As at the whole picture I look
I see young minds awaiting—what?
I wish I could say knowledge, but
I know they don't all want to learn.

It's hard to accurately discern
The needs they bring with them each day.
What can a teacher do or say
That makes a difference in their lives,
That helps them to set goals and strive?

Assignments they will need to do,
Questions they need answered, too;
Tests there are they'll have to take,
Decisions they will need to make.
How to all this am I tied?

Am I merely a student's guide
Leading them to information
To study for examination?
Or, am I a fact dispenser
Making them, each moment, tenser

About the things they must remember
To be for A's a true contender?
Or, am I a daytime sitter,
A monitor of teenage twitter,
Of disagreements, a referee?

How many of these can I be?
I must have lessons, quizzes, tests,
Activities, writing—do my best
To keep things graded and returned
So they can see the marks they've earned.

The time involved is overwhelming;
The task at hand is so compelling;
Not to dare to even mention
What it takes to keep their attention.
One must be an entertainer

Somewhat like a circus trainer.
O, Lord, I need your help to be
All these things and still be me;
And most of all I want each day
To touch each life in a lasting way.

I know to be that teacher true,
I must each moment look to you.

-1996

Life in Literature

For years I have admired the poetry of Dickinson;
I have enjoyed Masters' Spoon River epitaphs
and have marveled at how the play "Our Town" creates
appreciation of ordinary life.
I have taught this literature,
attempting to explain to students
how closely it all mirrors actual
life experiences.

Then, my daughter died,
and I had another semester in the school year.
It seemed that death took over...
in all the poems, stories, plays...
I had not realized how many of
Dickinson's poems were about death,
how much "Our Town" focused on the grave,
how even "Romeo and Juliet" could
remind me of my daughter.

I now can relate to students not just information about this
literature, but true understanding.
When I tell them now, they listen
in a different way because they know I know
what I am talking about.

I tell them that people write
about what touches them most;
that is why so many writings are of love, death, truth, beauty,
and so much writing is about
love and death
because these things we feel
most deeply
and they touch us all.

-1996

A Long Love Affair

On campus again---
nearly thirty years older
than the incoming freshmen
and still a student.

Walking along the tree-lined paths
from one academic building
to another

makes me want to be
a full-time college student once more.

A second chance...
at what?
my grades are better in graduate school
than they ever were.

Maybe it's the romance of...
being in love with learning—
infatuated with the process of research—
responding to the kisses of knowledge
and the caresses of insight.

Will it be a lifelong commitment?
Having been betrothed to books,
engaged in education,
will I, then, some day
be wedded to wisdom?

-1989
KSU

You Want to Write?

You want to write?
All right!
I'll help you put it into proper form.
You put your words on paper;
I'll tell you if they're warm, or cold.
But, if your thoughts are new, or old,
I may not know.

Of this I'm sure:
If your writing's strong or weak
I'll tell you so.

If your words are touching
I can tell.
If they say too much,
I'll say, "Well,
Maybe put that here,
Omit this there."
If they're not clear,
I'll help you find the words
To say what you want to say.
The thoughts are yours.
I'm just here to point the way
To proper punctuation and grammar,
To complete sentences, no stammer;
To clear expression of your heart,
I've had a little part.

The pictures that your words create
Come from deep within.
In capturing their essence
You show where you have been.

To really write with feeling,
You must put "self" aside,
And share your very soul in words
That cannot be denied.

You must be willing to allow
Others to see inside you.
Be ready for their scrutiny,
And then they will abide you.

Writing is an outlet;
It's a journey all its own.
So, let yourself go!
Let yourself know
How much you've really grown.

It's a record of where you've come from,
Who you are and where you're going.
Pick any part of all your life
Or thoughts and "let's get growing."

And you will find
As many have before,
As you keep thinking more and more;
As you create
Each new piece on paper
You'll feel so great
You will decide:
There's not much that's more exciting
Than writing!!

-1988

Exaggeration!!

Exaggeration! It's useful, you know,
To enhance the common; put on a great show!

You can add your ideas, whatever you choose,
To make tales convincing, to chase away blues.
You are the author, the holder of pen,
Who writes a great story again and again.

You'll create characters, evil and good,
Simple and complicated, just as you should,
Giving them interesting adventures and names,
Having them play many true-to-life games.

They may be people you actually know,
Or totally fabricated from the get-go.
They may be beautiful, sordid, aloof,
Mysterious, zany, accident proof,
Devious, genuine, innocent, pure,
Homely or humble, without real allure.

Your story can be serious, funny, or quaint.
It's all up to you what it is; what it ain't.
It can be very short, it can be quite long;
It can have chapters, it can end with a song.
It may take place in the future, the past,
The present, as long as the story can last.

It can teach a lesson or nothing at all,
Just mere entertainment like a fly on the wall,
But to be a good story, to have a real chance,
There are places which must be
Greatly stretched and enhanced.

The characters need to be larger than life---
Like Superman, Tarzan, or Mack with the knife;
Perhaps gentle like Ben or like Atticus Finch;
Mean like old Scrooge or that green thief, the Grinch.

Whatever the case, as the chapters unfold,
Imagination prevails till the story is told.
Adventure, excitement are the words of the hour
As suspense builds to give punch and power.

Nobody wants stories just like their life;
They want animation, more joy, even strife.
Readers want to go places they have not been,
And, sometimes, vicariously, to commit sin.

They wish to travel to places unknown;
To do things they never would try on their own.
To see things they might never actually see;
To be heroes or villains they never would be.

In order to do this, the story must tell
Of incidents entrancing and tell them so well.
If the action's too early or even too late,
The reader will lose the hook and the bait.

So----
As you, the author, proceed with your writing,
Make stories stimulating, lively, inviting,
One element's a must to receive an ovation:
Effectively utilize---Exaggeration!!

-2007

Goodbye, High School

Goodbye, High School.
My four years have reached an end.
And though I won't be back,
I'll long consider you a friend.

So long, High School.
It's time I travel on
To see what life will bring me
Before my time is gone.

Farewell, High School.
What I turn out to be
You can claim a share of
For you partly molded me.

Goodbye, High School.
My dreams all lie ahead.
I'm excited about my future
Wherever I'll be led.

My pathway may hold glory;
It may contain some strife.
But I'm ready! Goodbye,
High School, Hello Life!

-1974

Protected by the Promises---

---in Families

> Children, obey your parents in the Lord,
> for this is right. Honor your father and mother—
> which is the first commandment with promise—
> that it may go well with you and that you enjoy
> long life on the earth.
> --Ephesians 6:1-3 NIV

The Goal of Parenthood

To have a child and to watch him grow,

To teach him things that he ought to know,

To smile and be ready to understand,

To offer always an outstretched hand,

To guide his life in an upright way,

To be available night and day;

To be not just parent, but also friend,

From infancy to the journey's end;

To know that your child can look up to you

And see what is right for a person to do;

To feel that if you are put to test

You can honestly show you have done your best;

To see your child become someone good...

This is the ideal of parenthood.

-1966

DEAR GRANDPARENT……

A precious life, a tiny form,
So innocent and new,
A child to son or daughter,
A dear grandchild to you.
    Be it your first, or another of many,
    Each child's a special one,.
    As is every child who's born,
    As was your daughter or son.
        That this child has situations
        Which may seem quite unfair
        Simply means you're needed more
        To love, support, be there.
            Confusion, yes. Anger, probably,
            A feeling of helplessness,
            But this is a child, a life, a soul,
            Who needs your tenderness.
So Grandma, Grandpa, swallow hard
And find a way to be
The parent and grandparent that
You want this child to see.
    For these parents need to know
    That you'll reach out just the same
    As you would to any grandchild,
    Not casting any blame.
        And you may find as years go by
        The moments with this child
        Will be the dearest memories
        That you have been allowed.
            If you can look with only love
            At what can and can't be done,
            This child just may surprise us all-
            Your granddaughter, your grandson.
So welcome this, a precious life,
So innocent and new,
A child to son or daughter,
A dear grandchild to you.

                    -1990
        [when a child is born with a disability]

THOUGHTS OF A NEW MOTHER

I look into my baby's eyes and wonder what they see;
I realize that what he sees is really up to me.
I feel his tiny little hands and wonder what they'll touch.
The things that I allow him to learn will mean so much.
I watch him kick his little feet and wonder where they'll walk;
I hear his coos and babbling sounds and wonder how he'll talk.
For what he learns and what he does and says and where he goes
Largely will be up to me as any mother knows.

I hope that he will learn to see a pathway straight and true;
That he will show the way to go by helping others through.
I hope so much that he will touch the hearts of fellow men
By being the kind of person who's welcomed again and again.
And I hope he knows that where he goes, that where he takes his walks
Will say much more to everyone than when or how he talks.
He's my responsibility and the best way that I can,
I'll teach my little boy so that he'll grow to be a MAN.

And as I undertake this task, as I give him a "no" or a nod,
As he asks me questions, I'll ask my own questions of God.

-1966

Take Me By the Hand

Dear Lord...
Please take me by the hand,
Help me Thy will obey;
Let me fulfill Thy least command,
Don't let me go astray.

Help me to see Thy way is best,
And please help me to see
That faith leads to eternal rest,
Eternal peace with Thee.

-1959

Reflections of a Daughter

When I was two I looked at you and saw how big you were;
I thought to myself, "I will never be as big as her."

At age of four was even more a difference in our "size";
I tried to do things my own way—you made me realize

That age can have advantages and parents do know best;
But there's something about children that puts them to the test.

When I was eight was not too late to teach me many things;
That daughters should listen to mothers
or sometimes punishment "stings".

At age of twelve I found myself confused, stubborn and proud;
The things I thought I wanted most were those which weren't allowed.

At seventeen I had a dream and traveled far from home;
Then I was thankful for the guidance that my mom had always shown.

At twenty-one with college done, I commenced at teaching
And found that teachers, like mothers, never know whom they're reaching.

Past thirty now, for quite a while I've been a wife and mother,
And oh! How often I have thought of one thing or another

That from you I've learned; a bit of wisdom, a gentle touch,
An expression of concern that means so very much,

A smile when things seem low, a helping hand in need,
And at all times a ready prayer: these things have been your creed.

So, even though I've grown tall physically in stature, too;
It's in matters of heart and character
I'd hope to be as big as you.   -1977

At the Center of Generations

"I'm the center of five generations"
Every one of us can say.
Learning, teaching, enjoying
Each day along the way.

Valuable lessons for living,
Some purposeful, some not;
We all are lifetime students
Of lessons "taught" and "caught".

The things we learn from grandmas
Can't be taught by mothers,
And things we try to teach our kids
Are influenced by others.

We laugh, we cry, we "live and learn"
The comfortable and the strange;
We adjust because we must
As generations change.

The time is short as years roll by
From the moment of our birth
To becoming a mom, grandma, great-grandma
Before exiting this earth.

As a member of five generations,
At each stage I take a turn
To gain from the older to teach the young
With what that day can be learned.

We are all students and teachers
As we journey on life's way;
As a member of five generations,
What can you learn today?

-2002

THE ROAD AHEAD

The road ahead of them is long; its obstacles are high;
The reason they're succeeding is they're not afraid to try.
No matter what the effort that's required to succeed,
They push ahead, determined to satisfy each need.

Sometimes it's necessary that theirs is a slower pace,
But that does not prevent them from entering the race.
With handicaps and problems their lives are complicated,
But for each deficiency, it seems, somehow they've compensated.

To make up for their "quiet" legs, they've developed many charms
Like loving looks and dimples and Herculean arms.
They're clever little people, and more-than-average smart,
And if you're not real careful, they'll captivate your heart.

They manipulate those wheelchairs, braces, crutches, walkers,
Anywhere they want to go—and all of them are talkers!
Through countless operations, medications, casts, infections,
They "patiently" recover in spite of past reflections.

We wonder what their secret is of courage through it all,
Of faith they'll "make it somehow", though now and then
they fall.
They grit their teeth and all the while they're looking up above,
Perhaps that's why, with every breath, their lives exhibit love.

They take just one day at a time,
One step begins the miles,
And be the battle great or small,
They light the way with smiles.

-1975

What is Handicapped?

We have a little daughter whose body is not whole,
But that's no indication that she has less a soul.
She's a precious little person with a captivating smile
And a beguiling innocence that makes her life worthwhile.

Her legs are limp and lifeless; they're completely paralyzed;
But her arms are stronger than someone's twice her size.
She has determination that doesn't seem to quit
And deserves a lot of credit for the way she uses it.

She knows that Jesus loves her; she says He'll help her walk.
Her faith is sure and steady, such that no one can mock.
She wants to walk with crutches; her steps will come in parts.
The walking she is doing now is into people's hearts.

Her mind is ever-active; her eyes are sparkling bright;
Her voice is sweet and gentle; her actions, lady-like,
Her cherub face is glowing; her cheeks with dimples rippled.
She's the dearest "little lady" even though she's crippled.

Her hands are so expressive; her friendliness so apt
That I am moved to ask you, "Just what is 'handicapped'?"

-1973

My First Two-wheeler

Five years old—
    My first two-wheeler!

Dad held it steady
    as I learned to balance.
He ran along beside me,
    holding the back fender.

Over and over we practiced
    across the big front yard.

Wobbling and pedaling,
    I concentrated on not falling.

This time I was going
    farther than before;
I was into the neighbor's yard
    before I looked back
        and realized that
    Dad was standing
        where I had begun.

I was riding by myself!!
    Thanks, Dad!!

        -1993

Walking Tall

"Careful, now, or you'll fall flat,"
Dad warned
as we leaned against the house
and climbed onto the stilts
he had made for us.

"Balance is the trick,'
he cautioned.
Carefully, we "stepped" out,
on our tall peg legs, and
punctuated the grass
with square "footprints."

Sometimes we could walk
all around the yard;
others, we fell after
a few steps.

That lofty view,
however brief,
gave us a feeling of power
and accomplishment
as well as a glimpse
of what might be possible
if we have confidence
and follow instructions.

-1993

The Adventurer

My little son is only eight
But he's so busy here of late
I'm wondering if he'll soon be eighty,
His experiences are so weighty.

Already he's caught a thousand fish;
He's had occasion just to wish
He lived in places far and near.
It's not unusual to hear

His stories, never-ending it seems,
 Become replaced with far-off dreams.
He's a veteran pilot, a hunter, too;
There isn't much he doesn't do.

A trapper, a musician, singer,
A football player, always winner.
He's ever in a costume dressed
In order he may do his best.

He's so serious and well-informed
On each vocation he's performed.
His varied interests amaze me;
His stories of adventure daze me.

The little fellow has one crime:
His imagination's on overtime!

-1975

A Small Boy and a New Puppy

Eyes meet and instantly they know
together they should be.
The boy begs…"Please, Dad, please."
"Maybe," he replies. The boy says,
"He likes me."
They romp and roll and seem
to sense a unity of mind.
The dog looks longingly.
The boy says, "Dad, this is just the kind
of dog I always dreamed about
and wished I had."
The lady waits, hoping the pup
has found a loving home.
Dad says to boy, "Okay."
The boy yells, "Wow! He's mine! My own!"
And to the lady,
"You just gave a dog away!"

-1974

A Sober Reflection

I find myself
in the late afternoon
of my life…
Divorced
…not by choice,
by his insistence,
but a necessity for me
lest I, too, drown
in the deep pool
created by alcohol
and his dysfunctional decisions.

When I see him now,
I wonder,
midst the pain of viewing
the visible accumulation
of neglected health and
excessive drink,
if I ever knew this man.

Thirty-six years of marriage—
efforts, dreams, hopes,
forgiveness, exhortation,
compromise, ignorance—
all flushed away
like the yellow stream
of yesterday's beer.

His numerous visits to AA,
never accepting a sponsor--
five DUI citations,
impounded vehicles,
thousands of dollars in fines,
lawyers' fees, house arrests,
jail sentences, missed work,
lost jobs, deceived friends,
delusioned self, pleading
spouse, relentless son,
victimized daughter,
hundreds of "last chances"---
none enough to cause a desire
for rehabilitation, change,
sobriety, commitment.

So, while I face
an uncertain future,
sober, hurt, alone but for God,
he faces each day
denying his addiction,
a shell of who he ever was
or could have been,
ever thirsty
for the wrong things.

-2002

The Big Bad Wolf and the Sheep
(as told by a 19-year old)

> This poem and the two following were written when
> my son was a prodigal. This one I wrote as if he were talking.

I began a little lamb all clean and white as snow;
At first I stayed within the fold, for far I couldn't go.
I spent my time with other lambs or with my Mom and Dad;
I learned that there were rules in life concerning good and bad.

I knew the rules of my own fold; each one I tried to break.
I was a wayward little lamb and chances I would take.
My Mom taught me from early on that as I ventured out,
The world had many big, bad wolves just lurking all about.

She said they'd try to tempt me to do things that are wrong;
She told me not to listen to them or to their songs.
Mommy taught me about a Shepherd who loves sheep and lambs all;
That I should learn to follow Him and I should know His call.

She said if I'd but listen when facing a hard choice
That I would know just what to do if I knew the Shepherd's voice.
Well, as I grew I didn't listen to what my Mom had said;
I thought she was old-fashioned; I didn't use my head.

I saw her as the big, bad wolf and treated her as such
Forgetting she knew me oh, so well, and loved me oh, so much.

I found a group of black sheep and spent my time with them;
We got caught in painful brambles; all white sheep we'd condemn.
We blamed all of our problems on someone or something else
So we could have a "good old time" just doing for ourselves.

I thought I knew what I needed; I rejected those at home;
I didn't see what I was causing by my great desire to roam
From the sheep who taught me clearly so I could do what was right;
I ventured into further darkness; I refused to see the Light.

But my family kept on talking to the Shepherd up above;
They were following His directions; they were reaching out with love.
They were kind despite my hatred; they kept smiling through their tears;
They refused to give up on me through the weeks and months and years.

Now I'm far away from home thinking about it all.
I can see things much more clearly; I can hear the Shepherd's call.
I can see now that the big, bad wolf is the devil in disguise:
The world and its attractions pulling at me with their lies.

I am struggling to reject them and to turn toward the fold,
That the Shepherd in His mercy will warm me from the cold.
I know all sheep need a leader whether they are big or small,
But it is up to each sheep whether he will stand or fall.

The Shepherd loves each one so much, but we must make the choice
To let the Bad Wolf have us, or to heed the Shepherd's voice.

-1985

Climbing the Mountain---Slipping and Sliding

The prodigal son has returned to our home,
And although we didn't agree
That he quit in the middle of what he had started,
We welcomed him home joyfully.

The first month was like heaven, he so appreciated
Us and all we had done.
He told us, he showed us, how glad that he was
To be home and be happy, our son.

He carried in groceries, he helped with housework,
He willingly showed us he cared.
We had wonderful talks and enjoyed them so much
As his many adventures he shared.

Then he began to be discontent
With no job, no money, no car;
He now shows belligerence regularly
About what we expect, who we are.

I have prayed for his soul, for a job, for God's will,
I've reasoned and pleaded and cried;
But the limit seems to be two weeks at most
That he adheres to the rules we've applied.

Oh, Lord, I acknowledge that You are in charge,
And You're working Your will in His life.
I'm praying for patience to see this boy through
All the hatred, defiance and strife.

I've claimed him for you and I'm trying to give
You the freedom to do what You must;
To have this boy see what You'd have him to see
I know I must give up and trust.

It's so hard for a mother to see her own child
So confused by the world and its charms;
I want to just take him, as when he was three,
In my loving, protecting arms.

But he's made decisions that he knew were wrong
And he wants us to say they were right.
This family is so tired of the hassle
And wants to be done with this fight.

Oh, Lord, if I just knew what You want from me.
Should we help him with more than we have?
Or should we make him leave if he can't abide
By the few rules of conduct we gave?

He's so insecure; he needs to know love;
Yours and ours and his own.
Help us to help him find Your open arms
So he'll know he need not feel alone.

He's one of your sheep who is out of the fold;
I know You will search till he's in.
Help me do my part to help, not make harder
His seeing he must turn from sin.

I know I'm not patient enough, Lord,
But the past years have seemed a long climb.
I know there'll be victory at the top of the hill
If I take just one step at a time.

-1986

AMNESIA OF THE HEART

When you were a little boy, I held you on my lap
And read your favorite story books before you took your nap.
I answered all your questions, your whats and wheres and whys;
Your curiosity encompassed all that sits, walks, rides and flies.

I taught you to be honest; I urged you to be kind.
I let you make decisions so you'd learn to use your mind.
I gave you reasons for the rules, and love was number one.
Because we care about your life, we tried so hard, my son.

Your daddy took you with him in trucks, to games, to play in snow.
You love outdoors as he does; often fishing you would go.
You had friends and relatives who spent much time with you
Listening and playing, doing what you wanted to.

You had a dog named Festus, then Jack with droopy ears,
Then Max, your trusted buddy for eleven faithful years.
You played baseball and football; you tried basketball and golf.
At sports you were a natural, but you always just goofed off.

You had some childhood problems; headaches caused you pain;
Being hyperactive didn't help good behavior to gain.
You were such a delightful child with much potential there
To accomplish whatever you'd attempt in life, no matter where.

We went each week to Sunday School; you learned of Jesus' love.
You said your prayers each evening, and knew God was above.
You were always independent, and the rules you always tried,
But you learned that there was punishment if you purposely defied.

I look at you now at twenty-one; the hate you show to me;
The absence of respect at all; your language that's filthy;
Your total greed and selfishness when others are so giving.
I love you, but I hate the way this family has been living.

You tell me I was never there for you; your needs never met.
You say I didn't show you love; oh, how can you forget?
The love is here: you won't accept. My arms are open wide.
You reject me and cause us both to hurt so much inside.

I pray for your salvation. I try to be so kind.
I've come to the conclusion you are sick in heart and mind.
You want to live your own life, you say, but you don't try
To do what's necessary as the days and weeks go by.

You won't budget your money. You don't do your chores here.
You live by impulse daily and wonder what goes wrong, my dear.
I want so much to help you, but you won't cooperate.
I pray that something happens before it is too late.

I was not a decent mother, you scream. I feel the tears
And wonder who that dear child was I cared for all those years.
I've diagnosed your problem, at least the major part:
You've forgotten all the good things: it's amnesia of the heart.

I pray that you will realize that you must take the blame
For all the wrongs that you have done to cause a blemished name.
I hate to see you struggle more, but until you open your eyes
And have a desire to do what's right and stop allowing lies

To deceive you into thinking you are right and others wrong,
You'll keep yourself in darkness and you'll sing a sadder song.
I pray for your amnesia to be healed and then you'll see
That many people love you, and your responsibility

Is to be the man you can be. Only by God's tender grace
Can your heart recover and find its proper place.
I hope you'll wake up some day and know how much I've cared.
I thank God for your life even now and hope you will be spared
The agony you've caused for us. It can only go away
By surrendering your life to God, which I pray for every day.

-1987

> Thankfully, my son did accept the Lord, was baptized, and the last eight years of his life, he was a changed person.

Emotional Roller Coaster

I never enjoyed riding roller coasters
Even when I was a kid,
So why do you keep forcing me
To act as if I did?

    I hate the sudden changes,
    The jerking, halting ride,
    The knot in pit of stomach,
    The tightening inside.

It scares me that I can't get off
Until the ride is done;
It really takes me nowhere,
And it surely isn't fun.

    Sometimes I scream; sometimes I don't;
    But does it truly matter?
    No one can hear my heartbeat
    Above the constant clatter.

Onlookers think that all is fine,
That I'm doing what I choose;
They have no idea I hate it
Or what I stand to lose.

    There's no thrill in this ride for me
    Because you won't decide
    To ever be honest with yourself
    As you get on the ride.

You act like it's the only ride,
The only choice to make;
That the ups and downs are normal.
How much can one fool take?

    I know life must have valleys
    As well as mountain peaks,
    But there should be more smoothness
    If living's what you seek.

This nightmare is exhausting;
Its end is not in view;
I know I can make choices,
Why don't you know that, too?

    You can choose a different ride,
    A calmer, happier route
    Once you decide to realize
    What real living is about.   -1992

HOW HEALTHY IS HER LOVE

Some look at her with pity;
I can only see with pride,
For I'm looking at her little heart,
Not just on the outside.

Perhaps her body's crippled,
But how healthy is her love.
She's a little ray of sunshine
That we're not quite worthy of.

Through all trials she keeps smiling;
To each obstacle says, "I can."
She's a living, talking lesson
To each able-bodied man.

If she loves someone, she says so;
If she's asked to do, she tries.
You can usually find her busy
With a sparkle in her eyes.

Most folks would call her handicapped
Because her body's lame;
I see her as a person
And call her by her name.

For in our Father's blessed sight
I feel her life is whole;
She is using to the fullest
Her heart and mind and soul.

-1975

A Better Grandma?

I am calmer with my grandkids
Than I was with their father;
I'm more aware of what's important
And with what I shouldn't bother.

I'm as patient with my grandkids
As my grandma was with me.
Isn't it simply amazing
What I have come to be?

Is it that I have more time?
I'm ordinarily quite busy.
Perhaps I've realized it's futile
To "go into a tizzy."

I rather think it's that I've learned
Since my own kids were small
That time with children is precious
And that I can't "do it all."

It's a perspective on life that I see now
What's immediate and what can wait;
I take time to do things with people
Before it is too late.

I'm a much better grandma
Although a good mom, too;
There's just something about grandchildren
That brings out the best in you.

-2002

The Wedding Poem

Dear David ...

If I had looked a thousand years
    Or wished upon a star
Or searched the world for someone
    As special as you are,

I could not have found a man
    As wonderful as you
To care and share and laugh with,
    To discover love anew.

A man who seeks God's leading,
    Whose life's a daily prayer,
Who senses what is needed
    And is sure to be right there.

I thank God for the privilege
    Of becoming your wife;
I look forward to the blessings
    Of sharing the rest of life.

                Love, Jo Anne

Protected by the Promises---

---in Times of Death

Yea, though I walk through the valley
of the shadow of death, I will fear no evil;
for thou art with me; thy rod and thy staff,
they comfort me.
--Psalm 23:4 KJV

Death is a Reality

Death is a reality;
Yet it seems surreal.
To accept a person's gone
Creates a helpless feel.

The harshness of the loss
Takes time to settle in;
Convincing of the finality,
Where does one begin?

How does one stop thinking
The phone will ring and then
The voice you have been missing
Will speak to you again?

How does one stop looking
Out the window or the door,
Hoping to see that loved one
Come to visit just once more?

They say that time's the answer
To heal this awful wound;
Right now it seems impossible
That it could happen soon.

The brain processed the facts;
So why am I falling apart?
Perhaps because my loved one
Will never leave my heart.

-2010

Amy—

Your wheelchair is empty—
Your body is free!!
You are with our precious Jesus
Where we all long to be.

Our tears and our sadness
Are proof of our love—
Not sorrow for you;
You have risen above

The circumstances here—
All the problems of earth;
You bore your physical burden
From the day of your birth.

We consider it a privilege
To have loved and cared for you;
To share in such a special life—
To do what we could do.

We'll be with you again
When God calls us, too—
Until then—we will remember
All the days we shared with you.

Thank you for accepting
Who you were called to be.
Our love for you – in Jesus—
Is for eternity.

-1995

[written the morning after Amy's death-12/30/95]

BRETT, MY SON

A child who tested the limits,
A teen who surely rebelled,
A young adult, dangerous choices,
Multiple talents unexcelled.

Years wasted in selfish indulgence
Through which many diligently prayed
For return to the teachings of goodness
For Christ's love to be displayed.

A turning to God from the valley,
Commitment to begin anew,
Discipline exercised daily,
Determined in what he should do.

Reunion with three precious children,
A home in the country serene,
A job as a trucker…he did well,
A glimpse of success was seen.

Then…cancer…a horrible demon,
Robbed his body and earthly goals;
He valiantly fought through to victory—
For cancer cannot destroy souls!

-2009
(written several days after Brett's death)

1 Corinthians 15:57
But thanks be to God! He gives us the victory
through our Lord Jesus Christ.

Lessons Left Behind

(in the style of Robert Frost)

Whose grave this is I surely know;
It is my daughter's I loved so.
My only daughter, now at rest;
It was so hard to see her go.

Her life was difficult at best,
Paralyzed below the chest.
She struggled bravely through the years
Challenging each daily test.

I do not think of her with tears,
Moreso with memories which endear
The imprint that her life has wrought
On those who spent time with her here.

Lessons her existence taught
Are certainly with wisdom fraught,
And I am one who learned a lot;
And I am one who learned a lot.

-2008

He Knows Just How You Feel

"Oh, God! I've lost my teenage son!
He has been killed by fault of man.
It hurts so much to have him gone,
I don't want to go on. I can

See him as he used to be,
So full of life, so full of love,
And now he's gone so far from me.
Are you watching up above?

He was so young with so much ahead,
So much to do and give.
Why, God, why did he die now?
Why couldn't he have lived?

I'm grieving for myself, I know,
For you're in charge and you know best.
I'll handle what I can of grief
And give to You the rest."

"My child," said God, "If anyone
Knows how you feel, I do.
Remember I, too, had a Son
And gave Him up for you.

He, too, was young in earthly years,
He, too, had much to give.
I watched Him die a sinner's death
That those who've sinned might live.

It hurt me, too, to give Him up
To pain and hate and strife,
But I could see beyond His death
To His eternal life.

And you must, too, look further on;
Your son lives on, you see,
And through his death he's touched more lives
Than his life could have, for me.

Even your grief has caused more love
To reach out and to show
Than you can even imagine;
It's much more than you know.

I'm using you to demonstrate
That I can offer peace,
That through your tears and pain
Your love for me won't cease.

And just as my Son lives with me,
Some day you will renew
Life with your son on the other side
Where he'll be waiting for you.

So until then, remember,
That when to pray you bow or kneel,
You can always turn to me with all
For I know just how you feel."

-1986

Joyful Grief

I know the grief God must have felt
As Jesus cruelly died;
The sadness of His passing;
The tears God must have cried.

I now have walked that pathway
Of misery and pain;
Of giving up a child to death
I'll not see here again.

I've met God in the valley
Of the shadow dark and drear,
And in the midst of deepest woe,
His promises I hear.

The peace that truly passes
Understanding I have known,
And in the stillest hour of grief
I have not been alone.

But best of all, I've felt the joy
Of knowing she is free
And in His holy presence
For all eternity.

My spirit sings to realize
His every word is true,
And everything He asks of us,
He's walked that pathway, too.

I celebrate the victory
Of Jesus conquering sin
So we may choose to follow here
That we might enter in.

I'm glad the grave is not the end
And loved ones who have died*
Wait for us to join them
Where we'll all be glorified.

*died in Christ   -1996

Protected by the Promises---

---in Witnessing

And the gospel of the kingdom shall be preached in all the world for a witness unto all nations…
--Matthew 24:14 KJV

The Great Commission

Mark 16:15
Go ye into all the world, and preach the gospel to every creature.

Jesus told His followers, "Go into all the world and preach."
"But surely," you say, 'that can't mean me; that's too far out to reach."
"We can't ALL go," you rationalize; "then who would be left here?"
But scripture states it plainly. The message is so clear.

God meant that every person be taught about His plan
Of saving grace through Jesus that He offers to each man.
"So how," we ask, "can each of us fulfill this great request,
Taking the message everywhere. How can we do this best?"

Well, to begin, we can allow that our "world" is where we are;
So we can tell about God's love without traveling very far.
There's opportunity each day to talk to those we know:
Our friends, co-workers, neighbors, as on our way we go,

That salvation's plan is meant for all, and what they need to do,
And we can show them by our lives that we believe it, too.
Then, we can have a "mission heart" that's filled with loving care
For those who are in places far, teaching God's Word there.

We can hold their needs in prayer and do whatever we can
To support them as they minister in far and foreign lands.
We can send supplies and money; we can write to them and say
That we are remembering them and their needs in prayer each day.

For short mission trips to build and teach we can be involved in plans
To help raise funds, or actually go to lend our willing hands.
We can sacrifice some "extras' here to regularly and generously give
That work be done and that God's Son be known where'er men live.

So, you see, there's really no excuse to not be a missionary;
There are many things each of us can do God's Word to the world to carry.
Our hearts, our hands, our money, our minds, our love, our prayers
Can work together daily that God's love on earth be shared.

So now you know what you can do right here or traveling far;
To take God's message to the world, begin right where you are!

-1999-

The Christian Woman as Comforter

Did you ever know a woman
You could call on any time
And tell her, joy or sorrow,
Just whatever's on your mind?

A woman who can comfort
With a touch or just a word,
A woman who can smile in joy
At the wonders of her Lord.

A woman who is "always there"
No matter what the need;
Whose life is an example
Of the Galilean's creed.

You can tell her life is guided
By a special kind of care,
And that her inspiration comes
From practiced, daily prayer.

She never tires of serving;
Her loving knows no end.
If you know her, you are blessed
To have this Christian as a friend.

-1976

Reach Out, Christians

Don't just brighten the corner
Wherever you are;
Reach out to others, and
Let your light go far.

    Allow God to use you
    To reach others, too;
    Others who are where you've been
    Will listen to you.

        Tell them how you found
        The Way, the Truth, the Light;
        Tell it in their lingo
        If the situation's right.

Don't judge other people
By their clothes and looks only;
They know enough rejection;
They're tired of being lonely.

    Say, "Hey brother (or sister),
    Looks like you could use a friend."
    Listen to their story,
    Then help them in the end.

        Introduce them to your Savior;
        Let His light shine through you,
        So they will join the kingdom
        And have salvation, too.

'Cause Jesus died for all of us,
The cool and the uncool,
Let's love all those around us;
Let's live the Golden Rule.

    Let's live for Him who died for us;
    Keep others in your prayers.
    Let's show that God's the Answer
    When the question is "Who cares?"

-1994

GOD SPEAKS TO ME

God speaks to me;
I hear His voice when silence
Pervades my soul
And all around is still.

Amid life's noises
I can hear Him, too;
If you really want to hear Him,
Just listen! He will speak to you.

In times of sheer frustration,
He hears my plea.
He feels my contemplation,
He reaches out---and speaks to me.

I feel Him near
When I'm in deep despair.
I know He's listening
When I kneel in prayer.

I need but ask...
I know He'll send my needs.
I need but trust...
My hungry soul He feeds.

He is my strength in every single weakness;
He is my Hope through every passing day.
I turn to Him with everything in meekness;
I know He hears each word I have to say.

When I am plagued with constant worldly problems,
I turn to Him: He always sees me through.
Every time, He reaches out His hand,
Lifts me up and leads me what to do.

He is my friend; I tell Him all my troubles.
He listens well; I love Him totally.
That is why my Joy in life is doubled.
He'll speak to you just as He speaks to me.

-1976

THE BOOK WITH ALL THE ANSWERS

When I start to feel a little down, unwanted, all alone,
There is a book I open that has words for me alone.
It always says just what I need, has the answer to all things;
It is the Holy Bible. Oh, what comfort it can bring.

If I need to know I'm loved, I recall John 3:16.
It speaks when most I need it, and what God says, He means.
If I'm in need of comfort and things are bothering me,
I can find great solace as I read Psalm 23.

"Let not your heart be troubled," says John 14:1;
Jesus will take our burdens because He is God's Son.
There's so much in Philippians to help us on life's way;
I think of Philippians 4:13 at some time every day.

Chapter 4, verse 11 is another on which I depend,
And 4:19 tells me I always have what I really need in the end.
In 2 Corinthians 12, verse 9, I find that His grace is enough
For any problems in my life, no matter how crucial or tough.

I should try to help others when they're in need or dangers,
For Hebrews 13:2 points out that angels can travel as strangers.
I want to show my love to God and also to my neighbor
As commanded in Matthew 22, and I'll hope for rest from labor.

If I am faithful unto death, says Revelation 2, verse 10,
I will receive a crown of Life; on God's Word I can depend.
I am looking forward to the day all God's promises come true;
Until then I'll read His Word and do what I can do.

-1980

LIFE IS LIKE A FOOTBALL GAME

Life is like a football game, I just observed one day.
The terms in one apply to both as we travel on our way.
In both there is a goal to reach; a ball to carry far.
Sometimes we run, sometimes we kick according to where we are.

We manage somehow to gain some yards, then get tackled or blocked;
We try again to gain some ground; sometimes our heads get knocked.
There's plenty of interference, and always a referee
To monitor our progress, to watch us carefully.

We're at the line of scrimmage at different times and then,
Confusion and collision—and we fumble once again.
Sometimes we punt, sometimes we hike, at any rate we try
To make advances toward our goal as time goes ticking by.

We must remember always that we're a member of a team,
And though we can play solo, it's harder than it may seem.
The people on the sidelines will either cheer or boo,
But whether you keep playing is really up to you.

Sometimes offense, sometimes defense, up the field and down,
Kick or throw or carry to make points with a touchdown.
The game can be so rough and tough you think you just don't care.
Then, keep in mind the ball is just a pigskin filled with air.

So, always keep your goal in sight; fight to realize your dream;
And play to win each day or game to benefit your team.

-1995

FOG AND HIGHER GROUND

The fog was thick and heavy
   as I drove home late one night;
I could barely see two feet ahead;
   all else was out of sight.
I steered the car along the road,
   carefully inching along;
Seeming to make no progress,
   feeling the night's silent song.
After what seemed like a very long time
   the air began to clear;
The ground was higher and I could see
   quite far as well as near.

      The rest of the way was easy,
         with just patches of fog here and there
      in the "low spots." I realized all along
         I was under the Father's care.
      Isn't that how it is with life
         when you're searching for meaning and love?
      You feel "all closed in" by heavy fog,
         not seeing below or above.
      The world keeps you in the low spots,
         blinded to truth and light;
      You seem to make no progress;
         you feel you have dim sight.

            But if you find the Savior
               and give your life to Him,
            He'll lift you up to "higher ground"
               shedding light on all that's dim.
            There'll still be valleys and patches
               of fog from day to day,
            But you will know as on you go
               that your Father leads the way.
            You won't be dependent on your sight;
               you can rest completely on His.
            You'll wonder why you groped in the fog so long
     When He's where the Answer is.

                        -1982

LIFE IS A TEST

Life is a test, it's sometimes said. We study as we go.
What we learn is up to us, for there is much to know.

There are many kinds of tests a person has to take;
The more he pays attention, the better grades he'll make.

Morality is tested, as well as judgment, talent, vision.
How we score in each of them depends on our decision.

We must know which are true and false and which are multiple choice,
Which require an essay, and which allow a voice.

The test begins when we are born. Those we learn from have the power
To sway us to their own beliefs until we reach the hour

When we begin to know ourselves, to be able to sort things out;
Then we're responsible to choose what life is all about.

Some people are true students; some cheat and break the rules;
Some cram at the last minute; some go to different schools.

We continue learning so long as God gives breath;
We reach the end of earthly life which mortals label death.

And when we reach that Judgment Day, we'll stand before our Lord
And find out if we made the grade, or, of our own accord,

Failed to pass the biggest test which was, of all things, free:
Salvation by accepting Christ who died for you and me.

So remember on your journey toward that Judgment Day,
You cannot cram for the final exam: you must pass all the quizzes on the way.

                                                -1988

HIDE AND SEEK—READY OR NOT

Remember in those bygone years how we'd all play hide and seek?
The one named "it" would count out loud while pledging not to peek.
All would run and hide somewhere and "it" would try to find
Where each one was hiding: under, over, in, behind.
While "it" looked in one direction, there a chance would be
For someone in the other to run "home" and "get in free".

Some folks seem to think that they with God can play this game,
Not realizing that the rules are not at all the same.
They go and try to hide from God and think He'll seek them out
No matter what they're doing or what their lives are all about.
Or they think that He is counting and that some day there will be
A chance for them to run real hard and try to get in free.

The truth is, Home is where God is and He is waiting there
To see how many will accept the Son He sent to bear
Our sins upon a cruel cross that we might be cleansed anew.
The only way to "get in free" is to do what He said to do.
Believe, repent, confess His name, baptism, a life brand new.
These are the steps of salvation which He offers to each of you.

And as we run the race of life if to Him we look for all,
He'll guide, direct and lead us if upon His name we'll call.
And some grand day will be the hour when God tells Jesus---"Go."
"Go get my people, bring them Home; I want them here, you know."
Then, only those who've accepted Christ as Savior will go Home.
Hiding will not help when He says, "Ready or not—Here I come."

-1982

SALVATION IS A CHECK FROM THE BANK OF HEAVEN

I have a savings account since I have been saved
That never will run dry.
For He says in His Word that my every need
He can and will supply.

All my past sins He has cancelled, I know,
I can live from day to day;
And as long as I do not withdraw my Love,
He will guide and direct my way.

I have given the Master charge of my life
And the interest I pay is sweet;
It is Love, Peace and Joy in my life all my years
With a promise in Heaven we'll meet.

His resources are endless, abundant His loans,
Always open is His door.
So please tell everyone that by Jesus, God's Son,
They can be free evermore.

Now we know all have sinned, and the wages of sin
Are death and the devil and strife;
But we can live eternally in sweet victory
If we invest in the plan of Life!

Oh, salvation is a check from the Bank of Heaven
With your debts all marked fully paid.
For Christ paid it all when on Calvary He died
And in the dark tomb was laid.

But Praise God! He arose to bring to us all
If we will but receive.
All we are required is to open our hearts,
Then repent, confess, believe!

                              -1982

The Drama of Life

If we consider all the world a stage and each family a play,
Perhaps we'd see some reasons for the problems of today.
Each person is cast in a certain role which he doesn't always fill;
Some refuse to learn their lines; some only rehearse at will.

It takes discipline and compromise for the play to run as planned,
With the props, lights and staging each must lend a willing hand.

If there's conflict with the director, some don't show or miss their cues,
The play will not run smoothly; how sad will be reviews.
Some want the lead role always; others never want to lead;
Some seek always a supporting role to fill their need.

Another tragedy is when the actors know their parts,
But each is in a different play; this really tugs at hearts.
One may be in "As You Like It"; another "Romeo and Juliet";
A third, "Much Ado about Nothing"; and no one's needs are met.

Sometimes too much attention is paid to the play next door;
Then, instead of acting together, the family lacks more and more.

But when God is the director, and the man the head of house,
Then the cues are given right on time by husband or by spouse.
The children know their parts and lines as the acts and scenes unfold;
Just what their role is meant to be: the final curtain will be gold.

-1984

LIFE INSURANCE FOR MY SOUL

Do you have enough insurance? Are you covered, and your wife?
Do your children have assurance they'll be cared for all through life?
Do you have the proper coverage on each type of policy?
Mortgage and endowment, accident and liability?
On your car and home and self for you and family
you pay for years. Let me tell you what insurance is to me.

My money pays the due amount on me, the mortal man,
but my name's on the dotted line of the heaven-forever plan.
Repentance is the cost I pay, salvation is the key,
and Jesus paid my premium when He died on Calvary.
As an initiation, baptism made me whole
and bought a paid-up policy—life insurance for my soul.

I indicate my interest when I pray on bended knee,
and I have the calm assurance that I'll live eternally.
There's no other plan like this one, no other dividend so sweet.
The cost is small when after all the Savior I will meet.
He holds the mortgage on me; I pay-as-I-go with Love.
Through His grace I'll have a mansion when I get to Heaven above.

This wonderful insurance can also belong to you.
The question's not "Can I afford?" but "Can I afford not to?"

                                              -1976

MY FATHER IS BEST

Trying to "one-up" each other,
Two young boys argued at play
About their dads, whose was the best;
They were so young that summer day.

"My Dad's bigger," said the one.
"Maybe so, but mine is stronger."
Said the first, "But mine is smarter."
Replied the other, "Mine's been here longer."

"My Dad can fix anything."
"Oh, yeah! Well, mine's a teacher,
Knows the answer to everything."
The other said, "Mine is a preacher;

He knows God's word by heart."
"Well, my Dad daily prays
And he is always kind to others,
Helps them in so many ways."

And on it went; each of them saw
His daddy as the very best.
They grew and became fathers
And put themselves to test.

One day these boys met as men
And, as in days gone by,
They talked of fathers once again
Though both of theirs had died.

One said to other as of old,
"I have found a Father who
Can meet every need in life;
He'll always see you through."

"Where'd you find someone like that?"
"I found Him with my heart.
You can know Him like I do."
"Well, tell me how to start.

My life's been empty, discontent,
I call no man my brother.
I have no hope of happiness."
"Listen……" said the other.

"This Father's bigger than any man,
He's smarter and He's stronger.
He knows each of us by name
And He has been here longer

Than anyone who ever lived.
He calls us to turn to Him."
The other said, "How do I know
This is not just a whim?"

"Because, this Father's always kind;
He hears our daily prayers.
He gave His Son to die for us;
That's how much He cares.

For every soul He has created,
He has provided a way
For us to live for Him while we're here
And with Him some fine day.

He's a preacher and a teacher;
His word speaks loud and true.
His arms are open, reaching,
To welcome…..even you."

So now they're truly brothers;
They don't argue about dads any more
Because they share a Father
Who waits on eternity's shore.

With earthly dads and little boys
Or God in heaven above,
The common thread that binds us all
Is a Father's constant love.

-1994

A FULL CIRCLE OF LOVE

God loves everyone.
He Loves You.
He's Loved you from the
Moment of your birth.
He Loves so much
He sent His Son
To die upon this Earth.
And all that he asks
In return
Is that you accept
His Son
And follow Him.
Then you also
Will have Love for
Everyone.
That's a Full Circle
Of Love
Sent from Above.
-1982

I HAVE FOUND THE WAY

Whenever I have troubles
(they arise most every day),
I dismiss them all like bubbles
As I kneel again to pray.

One moment may be happy,
The next extremely sad;
But just turning to Jesus
Makes everything so glad!

Yes, no matter what arises
You can be sure I'll say,
"I'll give no thought to my tomorrow
Because I have found the Way!"
-1959

YOU ARE SEARCHING

*You are searching, my friend
I know what you're looking for.
The Lord has brought me to you;
He is knocking at your door.*

*He is waiting for your answer
So that He'll be able to give
You the peace that passes all
So in His Love you'll Live!*

*There's a vacuum within each of us
That only God can fill;
He doesn't enter uninvited,
Just when bid to by your will.*

*I am praying for you, my friend,
That Salvation you will find
So that you can have the rest
That comes with peace of mind.*

*I treasure so our friendship
And much deeper it will be
When you become my brother (sister)
Through the Christ of Galilee.*

*He is waiting for you, my friend;
His arms are open wide.
He knows your heart---He wants you
To let Him come inside.*

*Don't be fearful to surrender;
There is no need for fright.
He is Love and He can only
Lead you into what is right.*

*I know that it is worth it all;
Believe me, it is true.
This world does not have answers,
But your decision is up to you.*

-1982

The Lions and Lambs of Life

The lions in our lives can be
A source of fear and stress;
They roar and rage and interfere
And threaten happiness.

It's up to us to make a choice
To be brave or show our fear;
We need to take a stand for Christ
And all that we hold dear.

For Christ can close the lion's mouth
And calm the frightening roar.
He can give us opportunity
To faith and hope restore.

Yes, God the Father offers us
Entrance into His fold
By following our Shepherd
And obeying what we're told.

For Christ, the precious Lamb of God
Can grant us a release
From the raging, roaring enemy
And give us lasting peace.

-2002

Changing Only Me

Something I've realized, finally,
Is that the only one I can change is me.
I tend to set my expectations so high
That myself or others may try and try
And we all fall short, miserably.

I'm always trying to get so much done
I forget sometimes I am only one;
I try to accomplish what two or three
Could do if they worked together beautifully,
And I'm always on the run.

To accept others just the way they are
Is, in the long run, better by far.
I don't have to like everything they do;
I can love them and accept them, too,
So they feel they are up to par.

All the things I cannot tolerate;
Actions and attitudes that I hate,
I'll have to give them to the Lord.
I know that I cannot afford
To hold onto them and wait.

Oh, Lord, it is so hard to be
Content to work on only me.
I want so much to have things right
In your love and in your sight
I sometimes act impatiently.

Please help me, Lord, my love to show
So my friends and family will know
Though I have hopes they will go far,
I really love them as they are
And want to tell them so.

Let me walk so close to you
That everything I say or do
Will show your peace and joy and love
That each of them will look above
To want to know you that well, too.

                                                     -1986

THE GOSPEL ACCORDING TO HYMN

When I think of God's great Love, it overwhelms my heart;
I know THIS IS MY FATHER'S WORLD, I think HOW GREAT THOU ART.
Sing HOLY, HOLY, HOLY and PRAISES TO HIS NAME,
Because God gave His Son for us we'll never be the same.

For long ago one SILENT NIGHT a little town lay still,
WHILE SHEPHERDS WATCHED THEIR FLOCKS upon a nearby hill.
ANGELS FROM THE REALMS OF GLORY told of Jesus' birth,
As in a manger bed he lay, the Savior of the Earth.
WHAT CHILD IS THIS? some had to ask, not realizing then;
JOY TO THE WORLD sang those who knew He was the King of Men.

Christ's ministry on earth was brief, but the world knew He was here.
The life He lived while on this earth was an example clear.
LOVE LED HIM TO CALVARY. There JESUS PAID IT ALL.
AT THE CROSS....HE DIED FOR ME. He says I GAVE MY LIFE FOR THEE
What will you give for me?
HALLELUJAH, WHAT A SAVIOR, BLESSED REDEEMER of sin,
PRAISE HIM, PRAISE HIM with your life and let His love come in.

He did not stay within the tomb, CHRIST AROSE in victory.
HE LIVES! I KNOW THAT MY REDEEMER LIVES. He lives in me.
God planned a way through His dear Son for us to get to Heaven.
The steps to this salvation in His Blessed Word are given.
First, we must hear and understand THE WONDERFUL WORDS OF LIFE DIVINE.
OPEN MY EYES THAT I MAY SEE that EVERY PROMISE IN THE BOOK IS MINE.

BREAK THOU THE BREAD OF LIFE that I may ever know,
STANDING ON THE PROMISES is the way to forward go.
The second step, believing, causes me to say GLORY TO HIS NAME.
OH, HOW I LOVE JESUS; I'll never be the same.
LEAD ME TO CALVARY, Lord, JUST AS I AM, where I'll be saved
By the blood of Christ the precious Lamb.

Third, I'll ask forgiveness by GRACE GREATER THAN ALL OUR SIN.
MY SINS ARE BLOTTED OUT I KNOW when I let Jesus in.
Fourth, I must confess my love for Him; I must promise to TRUST AND OBEY;
I want to grow NEARER, STILL NEARER with every passing day.
INTO MY HEART I bid Him come. OH, LORD, I'M COMING HOME.
ON CHRIST THE SOLID ROCK I STAND, intending not to roam.

Fifth, in water I'M BURIED WITH CHRIST so my sins are washed away.
NOW I BELONG TO JESUS. Hallelujah! OH, HAPPY DAY!
I rise to walk in newness; TAKE MY LIFE AND LET IT BE.
AMAZING GRACE: GLORY TO HIS NAME, now CHRIST LIVETH IN ME.

THE HOLY SPIRIT enters one: THE COMFORTER HAS COME.
FILL ME NOW, I pray, and help me to lead others home.

I worship God in many ways IN THE SERVICE OF THE KING.
WE GIVE THEE BUT THINE OWN as tithes and offerings we bring.

TAKE TIME TO BE HOLY: Lord, TEACH ME TO PRAY.
I MUST TELL JESUS daily and listen to Him for the Way.
Submission...I SURRENDER ALL.
Communion...THIS DO IN REMEMBRANCE OF ME
Thankfulness...COUNT YOUR BLESSINGS:
HIS LOVE HAS LIFTED ME.

I'VE DISCOVERED THE WAY OF GLADNESS; I'm glad I BELONG TO THE KING.
IN MY HEART THERE RINGS A MELODY: IT IS WELL WITH MY SOUL I sing.

I LOVE TO TELL THE STORY of the BLESSED ASSURANCE He gives.
I'D RATHER HAVE JESUS than anything, and I am so glad that HE LIVES.
I'm only A SINNER SAVED BY GRACE who ONE DAY...LET HIM IN.
I LOVE HIM BECAUSE HE FIRST LOVED ME.
He came to save us all from sin.

I want to help RESCUE THE PERISHING;
Do you know I AM PRAYING FOR YOU?
I hope He will MAKE ME A BLESSING
As He gives me His work to do.

HEAVEN CAME DOWN FOR ME, brother, and you can have it, too.
The question is WHY DO YOU WAIT when you know what you need to do?
ONE DAY Jesus is COMING AGAIN to gather all of His own.
WILL JESUS FIND US WAITING for Him, or will some stand afraid and alone?

WHEN THE ROLL IS CALLED UP YONDER, I want to answer loud and clear;
WILL THERE BE ANY STARS IN MY CROWN, Lord?
It depends on what I've done for Him here.

                                            -1980

[there are 76 hymn titles in this poem]

When I Slip into a Valley

When I slip into a valley
And sometimes can't even pray,
My mind is talking, but my soul seems numb.
I try to "snap out of it,"
But it just won't go away.
I am searching, but the answer doesn't come.

Is this what you meant, Lord,
When you said, "By faith, not sight"?
Were you talking about times like these?
I continue to read Your Word
Though I can't "feel" the light;
I know You're there because You said You'd be.

And then that moment once again
I "feel" Your presence near,
And all is as I thought that it should be.
I'm tingling, bubbling, feeling pain,
Playing, laughing, crying tears,
And walking in the path You have for me.

"Be still my soul"…it has been still,
"And know that You are God"…I know,
That you are there no matter where I am.
When I am empty. You can fill,
You've promised joy to overflow,
I'm learning, Shepherd, to follow as your Lamb.

-1978

Free Gift

Anything offered for free these days
Is reason for suspicion.
We think it's too good to be true
And use our own ambition
To provide the things we want in life,
Not just the things we need,
When Jesus is the answer
If we will let Him lead.

It seems too simple to be true:
God sent His Son to die for sin.
If we ignore what He has done,
It's our fault for the shape we're in.
The thing that's hard to understand
Is that He waits for you and me
To accept the gift He has for us,
And only then will we be free.

Jesus paid it all
On the cross of Calvary
To take our sins away,
That's why salvation's free.

The gift is free,
You just must receive it.
To have it for your own
You have to believe it.

-1990

Unexpected Answers

We pray each day for many things;
We ask, and hope our prayers take wings,
That God will grant our greatest needs,
That we can plant in others, seeds
To grow according to His plan.

But, oh, He knows the heart of man,
And often in His wisdom, He,
Who sees what we're unable to see,
Sends answers of divine directing
That we are not at all expecting.

Yet, given time and put to test,
We find His answers always best.

-2003

Who's Following You?

Who's watching every move you make,
Your actions an example take?
Who's listening to each word you say,
So carefully its truth to weigh?
Who watches everywhere you go?
You may never know.

That's why so careful you must be
To have each deed that others see
Be upright, pure and wise and true
So they may know what's right to do.
Stumbling blocks making others fall
Won't do at all.

Your words must go with your behavior
That's why you need to let the Savior
Guide your will, your mind, your soul,
Your heart---to realize the goal:
That all desire to reach Heaven above:
You live His Love.

-1985

One Way or Round Trip?

If it's true that we all come from God
To earth for just a while,
And our final destination is
Beyond the sunset's smile;

If eternity is forever and
Two places there are to go:
Heaven and Hell, nowhere else,
This is what I want to know.

On our earthly journey
As we travel through the years,
Are we bound for Heaven's glory
Or a valley filled with tears?

The decision's up to each of us:
We make our travel plans
When we decide to bow to Satan
Or accept the Master's Hand.

We have the freedom while we live
To go where'er we please;
To stay at home or travel,
Work hard or live in ease.

But when we leave this body
To enter Eternity's door,
The conductor will be asking,
"Where's your ticket for?"

We will not need to answer;
The ticket will be marked
With Jesus' blood for Heaven
Or smoke for Satan's dark.

So we need to plan our journey
As each day follows day:
Round trip from Heaven to Heaven,
Or from Heaven to Hell, one way?

-1993

I used to fuss and fret and stew
Over things I couldn't do,
Or about what I wanted to
But could not.
I have found a better way
Since that all-important day
When I heard my Savior say
"Your cares I bought."

Yes, my life is so much easier
Since my days are filled with prayer,
Since I seek and find Him there
In His Word.
As I ask I find Him giving,
When I fail He is forgiving;
From now on I'll be living
For my Lord.

LIVING

FOR

THE

LORD

If I show love to my neighbor,
If I'm diligent in labor,
He will look on me with favor
This I know.
If I've given Him my heart and soul
And am baptized, I'll be made whole
And He will help me with it all
As on I go.

If you believe my story,
You no longer have to worry,
Do what He says and promised glory
You will find.
Even if you're Christian already
And still worry about things steadily,
You can have a deeper walk and sweet,
Sweet peace of mind.

Now my priorities are in order:
My LORD is at the top,
Then my husband, next my children,
Then my mama and my pop.
I give my burdens to Him;
I let Him be my guide.
I don't know where He'll lead me,
But I know He's by my side.

-1975

Seasons of the Christian Calendar

Each season's a reflection of God's abiding love;
He sends constant reminders descending from above.

Winter's dormant décor, frozen, frigid, cold,
Reminds us to create warmth for others to behold.
Snowflakes individual our uniqueness verifies;
Whitewonder beauty, a repast for our eyes.

Spring's refreshing newness gives hope to despair;
Birth and growth amazing after landscape bare.
Blossoms shouting color, buds to leaf diverging,
Glorious greens abundant, life indeed emerging.

Summer's luscious landscape, prolific growth surrounding,
Verdant pleasures indicate blessings sure abounding.
Gardens grow, producing nourishment for tables;
Picture-perfect produce which only God enables.

Autumn's artful palette is painted with such hues
That witnessing its richness our gratitude imbues.
Tapestries enchanting, growth advanced, mature,
Awaiting careful harvest, promised to endure.

The Christian walk has seasons much like the calendar year;
God's parallels have reasons which us to Him endear.
Our natural state finds us cold and frozen in our sin;
If we accept Christ's offer of a new life to begin,

Baptism, like spring rains washes pure and clean;
The Spirit comes to help us with things not easily seen.
We, like buds and flowers, grow stronger in His Word,
Opening and growing as His messages are heard.

Nurturing, like summer's sun and showers, makes us thrive,
Empowering us to witness that Jesus is alive!
Flourishing like autumn leaves, we age like soil's loam
Until the wondrous moment when the Father takes us home.

So, as you view the seasons, think of God's plan unique;
For the earth, for each of us, if His will we seek.

−2010

A NEW YEAR

Blink your eyes, it's here again,
Time to wish good cheer again.
Where did the past year just go?
Blown away like powdery snow?

Drifting down like autumn leaves
Skipping saucily in the breeze?
Burned by summer's blazing sun
Enjoyed by nearly everyone?

Now a new year extends before us
To sing a fresh and spring-like chorus
Of new beginnings, like the earth
Renews with life at each rebirth.

Look back—the old one's filled and gone.
Look forth—the new one stretches on
With empty pages simply waiting
To fill with much anticipating.

What will you do with the year ahead?
Face each day with hopeless dread?
Rush unthinkingly on through,
Thinking only of things to do?

Or take the time as you onward trod
To keep in tune and step with God.

-1995

Where is Spring?

Winter seemed so long this year;
I wished Spring early to be here.
I need sunshine to warm my soul,
To give me strength, to make me whole.

I long to watch the earth awake,
To know that there is no mistake
That Spring indubitably brings
A path to Summer's warmer things.

I have no doubt she will arrive;
It's just that I want to feel alive
By witnessing the glad rebirth
From Winter's dormant, frozen earth.

Spring's a temperamental Miss;
Perhaps she has been planning this,
So when she does decide to stay,
We'll glory in each lovely day.

-1996

Spring Cleaning

The lawns sport soft, new carpet;
flowerbeds are cleaning their closets
and wearing fashionable colors.

Trees sprout new hair styles;
all is scrubbed clean
by gentle rains and gusty breezes.

People pick up the clutter
of winter from their yards;
the hum of mowers vacuuming grass
fills the neighborhood.

Seeds and blossoms
dust the ground;
the area is polished,
prepared for summer!

-1991

Joy of Autumn

Autumn is like happiness...

Intense,
      Exhilarating,
            Breathtaking,
                  Vivid,
                        Yet fleeting...

But always worth the waiting,
For though so beautiful and brief,
We have the certain anticipation
That it will occur again.

-1974

Spring and New Life

Every year when we observe
The new life in the spring;
The plants, the trees, the earth renewed,
It gives us cause to sing.
    The debris of winter's swept away,
    All seems so fresh and new;
    The dead and dormant comes alive,
    Hope glistens in review.
        So recently the landscape
        Was frozen, barren, cold;
        Now we witness buds of life emerge
        Determined to unfold.
            This miracle's God's promise
            Despite a winter most severe
            Spring will always follow,
            There'll be a new song to hear.
        This process is a parallel
        To a life that's born anew
        In Christ's redeeming sacrifice
        He made for each of you.
    A person, dead in worldly sin,
    With hard and frozen heart,
    Barren of love and hope,
    With no warmth to impart
Can leave the winter of the world,
Step out of a life of sin
By accepting the promises of God,
Allowing Christ to enter in.
        Then hope shall spring eternal,
        Blossoms of love will grow;
        A new creation of the Lord,
        Evidence of change to show.
            Winter's debris cleaned from a heart
            That once was filled with sin;
            A purity the world can see
            Because Christ entered in.

Spring: a season to remind us
New life is a promise true;
Winter can be behind us
If we embrace what Christ can do.

                        -2001

Roots of Freedom

I'm thankful for my ancestors who left their native soil
For unknown challenges across the sea;
In efforts to escape persecution for beliefs,
They faced many dangers in hope of being free.

I'm grateful for the patriots who defied their king
To establish here a nation under God;
To have their independence, away from tyranny,
They fought for rights and settled on this sod.

I'm beholden to the soldiers from all the wars since then
Who put their lives in danger for our sake;
To keep our flag aflying and our country on its own,
They lived and died to keep justice awake.

I recognize the military in peaceful times and war
Who guard our freedom as we work and sleep;
Silent sentinels, alert to peril, always there,
Constant vigil of our country keep.

In addition to the physical, there is another war;
A spiritual battle for our souls.
A conflict between Satan and our supreme God,
Throughout all the centuries it rolls.

I give praise to Jesus who went to Calvary
Alone, so in our sinful need
We have hope of heaven if we choose to follow Him
Which allows us to be free, so free indeed.

This country is so blessed to have this heritage:
Freedom under flag and under cross.
Let us pay homage to God, the Giver of it all
Lest it becomes too late and all is lost.

America will not continue to be blessed
If it ignores the One who makes us free;
Let's look to Him so that these United States
Will always be a place of liberty!

-2010

SOME CHRISTIANS THINK IT'S HALLOWEEN ALL YEAR

Why don't you take your mask off, Christian,
Because God knows who you are,
And when it comes to fooling folks
You won't get very far.
Oh, you may have some thinking
That your faults are very few,
But there will come a time when
Your true self will be in view.
And then those you have falsely
Impressed will have a fall
To discover that you are not
What they thought you were at all.

Also, all that "church work"
That you find the time to do
Won't get you where you think it will
If you can be untrue
To family, friends and neighbors
When they need a loving touch,
And you don't have the time
Because you're involved in too much.

You see, being a Christian
Is not pretend at all;
It's all the way or nothing
When you answer Jesus' call.
It's not a part in a single play,
It's a life-time struggling role
With Jesus Christ the all-time star
And Heaven as the goal.

On this, our earthly journey
We need the world to see
The light of His love shining
Through the persons we can be.

So, take your mask off, Christian;
Submit yourself to Him.
Let Him guide and walk beside
And lead through bright and dim.
He can make your unmasked self,
Your deeds, your life, your tone,
So beautiful you'll wonder why
You ever tried to make it on your own.

-1982

HURRY-SCURRY CHRISTMAS

Already it's December which finds us in the midst
Of attempting every "have-to" on our Christmas list,
We hurry and we scurry as we valiantly aspire
To accomplish every item
To remember to invite 'em
To buy and make and bake
To craft and decorate
To sign and mail the cards
To deck with lights our yards
To wrap each gift just right
To fall in bed each night
Exhausted from it all, and we dare to call
This yearly experience a celebration higher than the worldly?

Joy and love and peace require us to cease
Hectic activity and concentrate on the celebrate.

We need to learn to discern the differences between:
Serving and doing,
Pushing and pursuing,
Acquiring and aspiring,
Assessing and blessing.

We need to learn to simplify
And truly try
To remember the holy night
The stars gave light.
The babe's arrival was not
In a palace, but a stable,
And only God was able
To provide the space:
A humble place.

So let's not get caught in
The rush among the throng
When He is all along
In hearts, not things,
And His love brings
Peace to those who recognize
The wonder lies
Not in the calendar days...but in the Praise.

-1993

The Best Gifts Give Ourselves

When Jesus came to earth that day,
Was placed upon a bed of hay,
He came to give Himself to us;
He didn't make a major fuss.
 So perhaps as we observe His birth
 While we are living here on earth,
 Instead of gifts purchased from shelves,
 We ought to give gifts of ourselves.
  That person who "has everything"
  May appreciate it if you bring,
  Not lovely wrapped gifts from a store,
  But something that means much, much more.
   An hour or so just spent together,
   A visit in inclement weather,
   A phone call when it's not expected,
   A note to say, "let's stay connected."
A patient listening ear can be
An answer to one's sanity;
An offer to run errands and such
If needed, means so very much.
 We can make Christmas last all year
 If we allow ourselves to hear
 The message from the Bible true…
 Don't just say, but also do!
  Time is precious, as we know,
  So let us love to others show;
  Let's have the courage to begin
  New traditions to usher in.
   Create joy by giving of your treasure:
   Time, hope and love no one can measure.
   Let's look for ways to truly give
   That Christ be honored by how we live.
Let's celebrate the babe born in a stable
By giving of ourselves as long as we're able.
Let's focus on the reason for His earthly birth,
And share in spreading His peace on earth!

           -2007

Scriptural Thanks Giving

On our calendars is a day in November designated for thanksgiving;
In our Bible is instruction that we were created for Thanks living;

Scriptures explain clearly the manner of giving praise to the Lord;
Repeatedly they offer a planner throughout God's Holy Word.

Through Jesus it is God's will in all circumstances to give thanks
(I Thess. 5:18)
For there are blessings He can instill even in tragedy's ranks.

We are to intercede for others each day along the way,
To request help for our brothers as we faithfully, thankfully, pray.
(I Tim. 2:1)

We are to enter His gates with thanksgiving and His courts with praise
(Psalm 100:4)
Giving thanks to Him for living, praising His name all of our days.

Jesus, our example, blessed the bread, the fish, the loaves, the wine;
We are to do the same, He said, being grateful all the time.

For those who travel far and wide the gospel truth to teach,
Pray they will not be denied that the unsaved they may reach. (Rom. 16:4)

Devote yourself always to prayer; offer praise for what you receive;
Of your example be aware that you live what you believe. (Col. 4:2)

Do not worry about anything; to God make your requests.
Before Him your petitions bring; He always knows what's best.
(Phil. 4:6)

Give thanks to the Lord, for He is good, as every Christian knows.
His love endures forever; our cups He overflows. (Psalm 106:1)

On Him our hope is ever set; to Him be given our praise.
The Victory's ours; never forget to be thankful all of our days.
(2 Cor. 1:11 and I Cor. 15:57)

Long before the November day designated to be Thanksgiving,
The Lord declared that we obey the scriptures in thanks-living!

-2009

MIGHTY NEIGHBORLY

A new family moved into town
so she went down
and welcomed them. She took a pie
and told them, "I
want you to know we're glad
to have you here." She had
a way of knowing what to do.
They said, "That's mighty neighborly of you."

    The man up the street passed away.
    She was there next day.
    Had already arranged for flowers,
    watched children during calling hours,
    had food ready when relatives came,
    offered a prayer in the parted's name.
    The out-of-town folks said, "Who's she?
    She sure is mighty neighborly."

        She did her own work cheerfully,
        and always had time for a cup of tea
        with a friend who dropped in "just to talk."
        Several times a week she'd walk
        across the town to visit
        a shut-in who would think, "Why is it
        she takes time for me?"
        The answer came—"She's neighborly."

At her funeral the preacher said,
with misty eyes and lowered head,
"When God said 'Love thy neighbor' she
heard and thought, 'why that means me.'
She practiced daily what I preach
and that's the only way to teach.
I'm sure He called her from her labor
'cause someone up there needs a neighbor."   -1970

ALPHABETICAL INDEX OF POEMS

                                                                                                           PAGE

Title	Page
A Better Grandma	50
A Full Circle of Love	76
A Long Love Affair	23
A New Year	88
A Revelation	16
A Small Boy and a New Puppy	40
A Sober Reflection	41
A Teacher's Role	20
Amnesia of the Heart	46
Amy…	55
At the Center of Generations	34
Brett, My Son	56
Caution: Detour	9
Changing Only Me	79
Climbing the Mountain…Slipping and Sliding	44
Cluttered Marriages	5
Collecting	6
Dear Grandparent	31
Death is a Reality	54
Emotional Roller Coaster	48
Exaggeration!!	26
Fog and Higher Ground	68
Free Gift	83
From a Teacher	18
God Speaks to Me	65
Goodbye High School	28
He Knows Just How You Feel	58
Hide and Seek	70
How Healthy is Her Love	49
Hurry, Scurry Christmas	94
I Have Found the Way	76
Joyful Grief	60
Joy of Autumn	90
Lessons Left Behind	57
Life in Literature	22
Life Insurance for my Soul	73
Life is a Test	69
Life is Like a Football Game	67
Life—A Dance Marathon	8
Living for the Lord	86
Mighty Neighborly	97
My Father is Best	74
My First Two-wheeler	37

Title	Page
One Way or Round Trip?	85
Parody	13
Reach Out, Christians	64
Recipe for a "Seasoned" Life	2
Reflections of a Daughter	33
Roots of Freedom	92
Salvation is a Check from the Bank of Heaven	71
Scriptural Thanks Giving	96
Seasons of the Christian Calendar	87
Some Christians Think It's Halloween All Year	93
Some Way to Walk	11
Spring and New Life	91
Spring Cleaning	90
Students of Today	19
Suffer the Children	11
Survival of Truth	14
Take Me By the Hand	32
Tell the Story? Why?	15
The Adventurer	39
The Best Gifts Give Ourselves	95
The Big, Bad Wolf and the Sheep	42
The Book with all the Answers	66
The Christian Woman as Comforter	63
The Drama of Life	72
The Goal of Parenthood	30
The Gospel According to Hymn	80
The Great Commission	62
The Lions and Lambs of Life	78
The Moon in Cancun	10
The Road Ahead	35
The Vicarious Gardener	12
The Wedding Poem	51
Thoughts of a New Mother	32
Unexpected Answers	84
Walking Tall	38
What is Handicapped?	36
When I Slip into a Valley	82
When Problems Pass Your Way	4
Where is Spring?	89
Who is ME?	3
Who is the Judge?	7
Who's Following You?	84
You are Searching	77
You Want to Write?	24